Money Management

Steps to Learn How to Organize Your Financial Life and Invest in Your Future.

© Copyright 2017 Connection Books Club
All Rights Reserved.

This document is presented with the desire to provide reliable, quality information about the topic in question and the facts discussed within. This Book is sold under the assumption that neither the publisher or the author should be asked to provide the services discussed within. If any discussion, professional or legal, is otherwise required a proper professional should be consulted.

The reproduction, duplication or transmission of any of the included information is considered illegal whether done in print or electronically. Creating a recorded copy or a secondary copy of this work is also prohibited unless the action of doing so is first cleared through the Publisher and condoned in writing. All rights reserved.

Any information contained in the following pages is considered accurate and truthful and that any liability through inattention or by any use or misuse of the topics discussed within falls solely on the reader. There are no cases in which the Publisher of this work can be held responsible or be asked to provide reparations for any loss of monetary gain or other damages which may be caused by following the presented information in any way shape or form.

The following information is presented purely for informative purposes and is therefore considered universal. The information presented within is done so without a contract or any other type of assurance as to its quality or validity.

Any trademarks which are used are done so without consent and any use of the same does not imply consent or permission was gained from the owner. Any trademarks or brands found within are purely used for clarification purposes and no owners are in anyway affiliated with this work.

Table of Contents

Introduction 1
Paying Less 4
Set Yourself Up for Success 12
Hold On To Your Money 20
An Active Approach 29
Investing In Your Future 34
Relationships And Money 39
Conclusion 45

Introduction

You have made a wise decision by downloading your personal copy of *Money Management: Learn how to Organize Your Financial Life and Invest in Your Future*. Thank you for doing so.

The following chapters will discuss some of the many methods for managing personal finances. As you read, it is important to keep in mind that no universal set of proven strategies for improving one's financial situation exists. However, this book aims to give readers the tools that they need in order to better their own unique respective scenarios.

You will discover exactly how important traits like diligence and dedication make themselves in the face of money management. Professional financial advisors are costly. For the price of this publication, you will obtain the knowledge necessary to increase your bank account balances and make marked improvements in your financial standing. Whether you want to pay off existing debts, save money, or simply develop an awareness regarding where your money goes, this book can help you achieve your goals that pertain to money management.

As you go through the contents of this book, keep the following consideration in the back of your mind. You will not experience betterments to your finances unless you do one thing: acquire more than you spend. If you can bring in more money than you pay, then, over time, your net worth will increase steadily. On the other hand, if your lifestyle costs you more money than you earn, then you are bound to fail at money management. The only surefire way to increase one's financial value is to establish a lifestyle in which the value of the money spent is less than that of all money acquired. Therefore, as you read through and begin to apply the suggestions found in this book's pages, do not lose sight of this goal. If, at any time, you find yourself considering an action that will leave you with an unneeded increase in expenses or a preventable decline in income, seriously weigh the benefits of that action against its financial implications.

The final chapter will explore the implications that romantic relationships bring to money management. When an individual gets married, their financial circumstances often change. Married individuals pay different tax rates than do their single counterparts. Furthermore, newlywed couples now have the responsibility of collaborating with one another in order to track the partnership's money.

There are plenty of books on this subject on the market, thanks again for choosing this one! Every effort was made to ensure it is full of as much useful information as possible. Please enjoy!

Thank you for your purchase of this eBook! I hope you enjoy reading this eBook as much as I enjoyed writing it. As part of your purchase, I invite you to join my email subscribers. This FREE subscription lets you receive a newsletter, highlighting the great new books available from Connection Books Club and other exclusive business and self development information. Subscribing is easy, and members receive great deals and fantastic eBooks at a discount! All you need to do is click this link to enter your email: http://www.connectionbooksclub.com/bonus/

Welcome to the club, and we hope you enjoy your purchase as well as our FREE newsletter invitation!

http://www.connectionbooksclub.com/bonus/

Prosperity is waiting for **YOU**!

Paying Less

Holding onto the money that you do have is an essential component of effective money management. Unfortunately, life necessitates that citizens of developed regions pay money in exchange for necessities like food, utilities, and transportation. In addition, taxes consume portions of taxpayer's incomes. This chapter will examine strategies for getting away with paying less on your bills and taxes. In addition, general tips for spending less money on necessities are included towards the chapter's end.

Paying The Bills

Bills are a source of contention for many individuals, couples, and families. Housemates may argue over who should pay what percentage of the monthly utility bill. A husband and wife might get into a disagreement regarding how to go about mortgaging their home. In any case, bills give people a reason not to check the mail on a daily basis. This section will examine how to save money on a variety of common household bills.

First and foremost, pay your bills on time! Failing to get your bills paid in a timely manner can result in costly late fees and interest. Worse yet, if you let a bill go unpaid long enough, debt collectors might start showing up in your life, sending you into an even more disorganized financial state. Submitting payments for your bills on time will help you become more financially organized. Remember that once a bill is paid, you no longer have to worry about it. Of course, you should know when to expect recurring bills such as utilities and rent. However, one-time bills like those from a hospital will be settled and behind you, once you get them paid. Know that paying your bills on or before their respective due dates will benefit you in the long run by saving you money on late fees and keeping you up-to-date on your financial obligations.

Second, try saving money on your home heating bill. If you have an attic in your home, make sure that your attic is well-insulated; most of the heat that escapes from your home will leak out through the attic. Having a well-insulated home will help you save money on home heating costs. Furthermore, you can get away with not running the heater at all. It is very easy to get accustomed to sleeping in cold temperatures. I live along the coast of Northern California where temperatures often linger just above freezing throughout the night. My roommates and I, in an attempt to save on our home heating bill, bundle ourselves up under heavy blankets (not the same ones, mind you) while we sleep. If we get cold before bedtime, we just put on more clothes. A willingness to bundle up in your own home will save you hundreds if not thousands in home heating costs over the course of one year.

Third, you can save a considerable sum of money on your water heating bill by taking a few steps. Namely, insulate your water heater and opt to do laundry using the cold cycle. If your water heater is well insulated, then you will consume less energy keeping its contents hot. In turn, you will spend less on energy bills. Search online for a "water heater jacket" and consider purchasing one for your make and model. In addition, you will save money on water heating if you launder your dirty garments using your washer's "cold" setting. When you set your washer to run on cold, you will not use additional energy to heat your laundry's water. The only energy that your washer will consume will be used to power the machine itself. It is estimated that a modern washing machine's hot cycle burns more than twenty times as much energy as its cold cycle.

Fourth, your credit card bills and the ways in which you handle them will play a huge role in determining your financial situation. As such, it is important to exercise caution when using a credit card. You do not need to keep a perpetual balance on your credit card in order to establish a favorable credit rating. In fact, doing so is not recommended; overdue credit card balances are likely to accumulate interest. In order to build credit using a credit card, you only need to make purchases with it, and then pay those purchases off in a timely manner. You can pay off your credit card balance on the same day that you acquire it and you will still build credit. Thankfully, most major contemporary financial institutions and banks offer consumers the convenient option of paying their credit card bills using a website or smartphone app. If you have credit card debt that you cannot pay off by its due date, see if you can transfer that balance to a card with a lower interest rate.

Taxes

Unfortunately, in most developed nations, taxes are as inevitable as death. The governments that govern functioning civilizations need monetary funds. They obtain that money by collecting taxes from citizens. This section is designed to help readers survive the ever-present burden known as taxes.

First, if you live in the United States, you will be paying your federal taxes to an organization called the Internal Revenue

Service. Often abbreviated as the IRS, this institution is responsible for collecting and recording tax payments from American citizens. According to their own website, the IRS does not find cash to be an acceptable form of payment when it comes to taxes. Issues with counterfeit bills and the fact that cash is hard to track make that form of payment unattractive to them. They would prefer to receive a check made out to United States Treasury. The IRS also accepts electronic withdrawals and credit cards. You can make payments directly through their website, IRS.gov.

Next, make sure to pay your taxes in full before their due date. If you are late on your taxes, the organization in charge of collecting that revenue will likely charge you a late fee. This penalty can add up fast, too. Initially, you will be charged five percent of the amount that you owe. If you procrastinate on paying your taxes too much, you could find yourself facing a penalty equal to one hundred percent of the original amount owed. In most cases, however, the government will not send collectors to your doorstep if you fall behind in your tax payments. They reserve that collection method for serious tax evaders only. Still, your financial situation will not improve unless you have all of your taxes paid on time. A later chapter will cover budgeting and setting aside money for obligatory expenses like taxes.

In the event that you find yourself unable to pay your federal taxes in a timely manner, do not try to escape that responsibility. The IRS will not forget about you if you ignore them long enough. Instead, contact the IRS and see if they will be willing to work with you. Many Americans have successfully worked out an agreement with the IRS that satisfied both parties and kept the individuals in good standing with the service. Contingent on your personal financial situation, the IRS may be willing to subsidize a portion of your debt, work out a payment plan, forgive your debt entirely, or even give you money.

Along those same lines, you may be considering the benefits of a tax preparer. A tax preparer is a professional individual who specializes in the preparation of other people's tax documents. Utilizing the services of a tax preparer will save you time and effort. In addition, having an expert go over your tax returns helps ensure that you save as much money as possible on this burdensome expense. However, tax preparers usually charge for their services, so you will have to factor in the cost of hiring one when determining if their services might be worthwhile for you and your unique situation.

If you miss the due date on your federal taxes, the IRS will be willing to negotiate a repayment schedule with you. Under this agreement, you will have to diligently make regular payments until your balance is paid off. Be warned that the IRS does not tolerate missed or late payments on a repayment schedule. If you get your monthly repayment in after its due date or fail to submit it entirely, you will have defaulted on your repayment schedule. If that happens, you and the IRS will have to once again try to negotiate a repayment schedule after you have already proven yourself unreliable.

Finally, if you and the IRS are simply unable to come to an agreement regarding the status of your federal taxes, you should know your rights. Specifically, as a taxpayer, you possess the right to have an attorney represent your case and you. A tax attorney who knows the nuances of the nation's tax laws can help you get the best possible deal with the IRS.

The cost of a tax attorney's services might outweigh the cons of battling the IRS alone. Your unique situation will determine the right steps for proceeding with paying taxes.

Spending Wisely

If you spend your money wisely, you will be left with more money at the end of your shopping cycle. This section will provide readers with tips and suggestions for spending money in a wise fashion on a variety of common purchases, including groceries and gasoline.

First, in order to spend money wisely, you must pledge to only spend money on needs. Needs are the things that you cannot sustain a comfortable life without. They include shelter, nourishment, hydration, transportation, toiletries, and the like. On the other hand, you should avoid spending money on wants. Wants, as opposed to needs, do not make themselves necessary ever. Wants include luxury goods like jewelry, vices like tobacco, superfluous add-ons like custom speakers for your car, and top-dollar cosmetics. Groceries from the basic food groups are needs; five-star restaurant meals are wants. Needs should consume an overwhelming majority of your spending budget.

Second, the grocery store can eat into your spending money if you do not shop wisely. Grocery stores are designed to make shoppers walk through as much surface area of the store's floor as possible. To illustrate, think about the last major corporate grocery store that you visited. If the store's interior designers were savvy, they likely placed grocery essentials like bread, dairy products, meat, and fresh produce along the store's perimeter, as far away from one another as possible. In doing so, they hope that customers will cross through the center of the store and expose themselves to unneeded items as they walk to each of the sections containing the typical grocery necessities. In order to help yourself avoid temptation and only stick to what you need, start your trip to the grocery store by walking along the store's perimeter. Avoid going into the centrally located aisles until you have gotten everything that you need from the store's outskirts.

Along those same lines, sign up for grocery store rewards cards. These free programs allow shoppers to pay lower "members only" prices on certain items throughout the week. Of course, use coupons, but only on items that you were planning on buying anyways. Do not spend money on junk foods that provide little to no nutritional value. Opt for healthy, wholesome choices and fill your cart with them. Buy in bulk, but only when it makes sense to do so. For example, do not buy the pack of three gallons of milk if you will struggle to finish two by the time that they expire. If you can stomach a generic product or find little difference between generic and name-brand, opt for the less expensive of the two. If you find an item at a great temporary price that you know that you will use before it goes bad, stock up on it. Lastly, make use of the smartphone apps Checkout 51, Ibotta, Groupon Coupons, Saving Star to earn cash back on groceries.

Third, gasoline, while unreasonably expensive, does not have to consume your budget like your SUV consumes gasoline. When you fill up, fill up your tank all the way so that you do not have to use more gasoline prematurely diverting yourself to the gas station again in the near future. Wait until your vehicle is almost out of gasoline before you buy more; the less gasoline you have in your gas tank, the less your car will weigh. Lighter vehicles burn less gasoline than heavier ones. Furthermore, consider signing up for a fuel rewards program. Many major corporate gasoline companies offer consumers money-saving deals in exchange for brand loyalty. Drive with your windows up; open windows create wind resistance, a phenomenon known to waste fuel. In addition, if you keep your tires inflated to almost their maximum PSI, you will get better gas mileage than you would if you drove on poorly inflated rubber wheels. Finally, do not drive with your vehicle's climate control on. The air conditioners and heaters found inside of vehicles use gasoline to operate; turning them off will save your fuel.

In sum, you will have to spend money if you are going to obtain necessities and the fuel for transporting yourself to your place of employment, the organization that provides your primary source of income. However, if you are diligent and aware, you stand to save a great sum of money on these nearly unavoidable expenses.

Enjoying your eBook so far? Take a moment to subscribe to our FREE newsletter for incredible discounts, books giveaways, and VIP offers!

> http://www.connectionbooksclub.com/bonus/

All we need is your email, and you'll be set up to receive more of the eBooks you can't wait to read.

Set Yourself Up for Success

In order to succeed financially, you cannot have any outstanding debts or be disorganized. It is my hope that my readers find themselves able to navigate their respective financial scenarios independently. As such, this chapter will help readers manage debts and tend to their own senses of financial organization.

Managing Debt

Debt is unforgiving. If you are timely with all of your mandated payments, then debt probably does not haunt you. However, if you are behind on payments or struggling to keep up with them, then you will want to follow the tips in this section for managing debt.

Managing debts is a matter of prioritization. In most cases, you will want to prioritize paying off the debt that is generating the most interest and fees. For example, if you owe the same amounts of money on two different credit cards with differing interest rates, consider which card is costing you more. If card 1 has an interest rate of twenty percent while card two charges an interest rate equal to ten percent, it makes sense to focus on paying off card 1 first while making the minimum payment on card 2. Experts insist that the most effective way to pay off multiple credit cards involves making lump sum payments on only one card at a time. In addition, never neglect to make a minimum monthly payment; to do so would be disastrous for your financial life.

On the other hand, it may be of a psychological benefit to pay off the smallest credit card debt before shifting your attention to the larger balances. Formerly bankrupt millionaire David Ramsey says that he received motivation when he paid off a debt, no matter how small. He recommends that individuals experiencing intense feelings of overwhelm pertaining to their debts start their journey towards financial stability by paying off any lingering, affordable debts first. The remaining debts will seem more manageable, simply because there are less of them in total, despite the fact that the amount owed is larger than it would be if one large debt had been prioritized. Ultimately, you will have to decide if the psychological edge gained from quickly paying off one debt is worth the extra interest fees.

Additionally, some past-due accounts go to a collections agency. When an organization does not receive money owed in what they deem a timely manner, they have the right to send that account to an independent organization responsible for obtaining the money for them. In other words, if you fail to pay your bills on time, you might find yourself in contention with a collections agency. Unfortunately, failure to pay the collections agency within a given period of time, usually sixty days, will affect your credit score in a negative way. As such, if you have some accounts in collections and others that are in good standing, it will benefit you in the long run to pay off your accounts that are not in the hands of a collections agency first, before you make large payments towards those that have gone to collections. This will prevent other debts from affecting your credit score in addition to the ones that already do.

Another option for debt management comes in the form of a settlement. If you owe an outstanding balance on your credit card, you might be able to settle with the credit card company for less than the original balance. Not all companies will be willing to settle, but some will be happy to take a portion of the balance and forgive the rest so that they can stop using resources while trying to collect what you owe them. Call your credit card company and ask to speak to somebody qualified to negotiate a debt settlement. It will help your case if you are prepared to make a lump sum payment or establish a very short-term payment plan. Be warned, however, that the credit card company may wish to cancel your card or lower your credit limit as a term of the settlement.

If you are currently facing high-interest debts from a variety of sources, then a debt consolidation loan would be worth considering. For example, one might owe money on their multiple credit card, hospital, and utility bills. Debt consolidation loans are intended for individuals owing money to various institutions.

Under the terms of such an agreement, a wealthy creditor agrees to pay off the remainder of the debtor's outstanding balances, saving the debtor some money on the future accrual of interest. In exchange, the debtor pays the creditor back with regular monthly payments until the original balance of the debts plus the creditor's interest rate is paid off. The creditor collects interest from the debtor in an amount less than what the debtor would have paid to the original sources of his or her debts.

Well-meaning individuals report a number of positive benefits from debt consolidation loans. Namely, they save money on interest. Additionally, a debt consolidation loan will, in most cases, reduce the number of collections calls that a debtor receives. Furthermore, the debtors' respective credit scores get preserved, provided that they make timely payments to the creditor. One of many debt management options, a debt consolidations loan works by combining all of an individual's outstanding debts into one single lump sum debt.

Next, bankruptcy is another one of your options for managing debts. Contrary to popular misbelief, a declaration of bankruptcy will not immunize you from your outstanding debts. Rather, when a court grants you the right to declare bankruptcy, you will still be expected to pay back every dollar that you owe. However, you will receive protection from the federal court systems while you repay all of the money that you owe. The two most common types of bankruptcy filings, Chapter 7 and Chapter 13, each provide debtors with a different way of paying off debts.

Chapter 7 bankruptcy filings, in most cases, call for the debtor to pay off their debts within six months or less. However, they are not required to use cash in order to make their payments. Under the terms of a Chapter 7 filing, the debtor may choose to sell, or liquidate, his or her valuable items and assets. Then, the money earned from the sale of those possessions goes towards paying off the money that is owed to the creditors. The courts will determine which possessions should be sold so that debtor's loss of assets is appropriate for his or her situation.

In some cases, you may get to retain the majority or even the entirety of your estate. Certain items are federally exempt from Chapter 7 bankruptcy law. Each state has different laws pertaining to the types of assets that might be exempt from a Chapter 7 filing. If you meet your state's criteria, you might be surprised to discover that you can hold onto one hundred percent of your possessions and still be granted a bankruptcy.

On the other hand, if you earn regular wages, then you likely qualify for a Chapter 13 filing. If you can provide the courts proof, such as a paystub, of your income, then you should consider filing for a Chapter 13 bankruptcy. Under the terms of such an agreement, the debtor provides a detailed payment plan that outlines how they intend to pay off their remaining debts. If the judge deems that the applicant will have the ability to live up to the terms of their own proposal, then the debtor will receive a Chapter 13 bankruptcy, which comes with federal protection from further harassment from debt collectors.

Financial Organization

Organizing your finances and all pertinent documents and files will be of immense help in crafting your monthly budget, which will be discussed in detail in the next chapter. For now, you should focus on getting all of your paperwork in order. Organization is essential; if you lose track of your outstanding bills, you can find yourself facing unexpected monetary penalties in the forms of interest and late fees. You probably do not have to utilize every suggestion in this section in order to organize your finances. However, I recommend that you choose the tips that apply to your unique situation so that you might come up with a working system that effectively organizes your finances.

First, stay on top of your bills. Collect the contents of your mailbox on a daily basis. As soon as you receive a bill in the mail, open it. It may be unpleasant to look at the outstanding balance on your bill, but procrastinating on that experience will not do you any good. Then, if you have the means to do so, pay that bill immediately. You can then check that bill off of your mental or tangible list of financial responsibilities and forget about it.

Similarly, keep up with your bills by generating a three-columned list of bills. This is not to be confused with the three-columned budget that will be discussed in the next chapter. In the column on the far left of your bills list, write down all of the bills that you expect to receive in a given month. For now, do not worry so much about the dollar amount that you expect to see on that bill; just write the names of the bills themselves, such as "utilities" or "car insurance." Then, in the middle column, write down the names of the bills that you receive as you receive them, along with the dates that you receive each bill and their respective due dates. Finally, in the third column, write down the name of each bill as soon as you pay it, along with the date that you send the payment. In the event that you and a company or creditor get into a dispute regarding one of your bills, you will have your list to refer to. Furthermore, you will not be left wondering whether you need to still need to set aside money for your credit card bill or not, for example.

Next, you will want to have a physically organized stack of bills and expenses. Keep all of your bills in the same place. Perhaps you set aside a desk drawer, a folder in a file cabinet, or a tier on a stacking tray. In any case, keeping all of your bills in one physical location will prevent you from scrambling to find records of any one bill when you need it. If you receive bills electronically, keep all of your bills organized in one file folder or email folder. Subfolders are absolutely okay as well, so long as you have one overarching folder that hosts them all. Similarly, you are free to subdivide or subcategorize your physical copies of bills within their master location as well.

If technology appeals to you, consider making use of professional financial software. Many pieces of financial software are designed to help users organize their respective financial lives. In addition, a simple excel spreadsheet can help most people stay financially organized.

Moving along, some financial experts recommend having two checking accounts in order to better organize their finances. They suggest having one account for necessary spending and the other for discretionary spending. You should aim to keep the balance of your necessary spending account high enough to cover all of your mandatory expenses for the month. Your other account is for fun. For example, if you go out for drinks with friends, having a second account for discretionary spending will help prevent you from spending your utility bill money on alcohol. It is recommended that you do not take the debit card tied to your necessary spending checking account out of your home. Some people go so far as to cut up that card, leaving only the numbers intact so that they can make online bill payments with it.

In the event that you and a partner, spouse, or family member share an account, the need to stay organized gets even stronger. Not only are you responsible for your own spending, saving, and budgeting habits, but you also have to keep tabs on somebody else's. If you are unaware of how much the other person linked to your account has spent, you might accidentally overdraft the account. Owners of a shared account should regularly communicate with one another regarding finances that pertain to that account. Furthermore, the two of you should definitely consult before one makes a large purchase.

Also, individuals enrolled in direct deposit should ensure that their paychecks always arrive in the corresponding account on time. When you expect that your directly deposited paycheck has arrived, check the balance on the linked account so that you do not unknowingly spend more money than you have in your account. Doing so could lead to overdraft fees, despite the pending arrival of your next paycheck. It is fairly common for incoming money to a bank account to get put on hold until the bank verifies its legitimacy. A quick check up on your balance every payday could save you stress and money.

Next, once your budget is established, you should refer to it before making any weighty financial decision. Although the budget plan discussed in the next chapter is aimed at guiding users through their financial situations on a month-to-month basis, you should be checking it more frequently than once every thirty days. If you are going to stay organized, you will have to regularly update your budget and make any necessary adaptations.

Finally, hold on to every financial document that you receive. Keep them organized in one place. Do not discard any receipts, pay stubs, bills, I.O.U.s, any other documents that reflect your spending and earnings.

Enjoying your eBook so far? Take a moment to subscribe to our FREE newsletter for incredible discounts, books giveaways, and VIP offers!

- http://www.connectionbooksclub.com/bonus/

All we need is your email, and you'll be set up to receive more of the eBooks you can't wait to read.

Hold On To Your Money

If an individual intends to pay off existing debts, build wealth, or otherwise improve their own financial situation, then that person cannot avoid the fact that they must acquire more money than they spend or lose. As such, it will be in your best interest to focus your efforts on spending money at a rate that is slower than the speed at which you accumulate it. In other words, the most financially successful businesses, organizations, and individual persons around the world all have one thing in common: they bring in more money than they spend. Budgeting and saving will greatly assist you in your journey towards that end. These processes require diligence and discipline, but financial stability does not come to the unwilling.

Budgeting

A budget will help you keep track of your finances. This section will cover the essential features of a budget. In order to create your budget, you must have a way to track your monthly expenses and incomes. As such, hold on to your receipts, bills, pay stubs, and any other documentation of financial costs and monetary earnings.

Start your budget by creating a three-columned list. Do not mistake your three-columned budget for your three-columned bill tracking system discussed in the previous chapter. Use the medium that feels most comfortable to you and your lifestyle. Some individuals make use of computer software; others prefer handwritten budgets using media such as plain paper and pen. Budgeting smartphone apps also exist. Seasoned budgeters recommend using a large dry erase board so that any variable items can be erased, adjusted, and adapted to as they change and that the budget will be highly visible. You may have to experiment with different budget media until you find one that you like.

In the column on the left, create an itemized list of all of your fixed expenses. Your fixed expenses are the costs that you anticipate paying on a regular basis and in equal sums of money each month. Examples of common fixed expenses include rent, property taxes, garbage collection bills, installments on hospital bills, union dues, and so on. Fixed expenses are predictable, unavoidable lest a major change occurs in your life, and recurring, either in perpetuity or not. As mentioned earlier, it is essential that you keep track of all of your receipts and bills for this portion of the budget creation process. The accuracy of your budget depends on it. When you have taken exhaustive inventory of all of your fixed expenses and listed each one along with its corresponding dollar amount, add up the total sum of the dollar amounts on this list. Continuing to move vertically down your left column, leave a blank space and then make an entry that reads TOTAL: $[Sum of fixed expenses].

You might find that you have predictable, fixed expenses that recur less frequently than once a month, including car insurance, dental bills, and quarterly donations. If that is the case, calculate the average monthly cost of these less frequent fixed expenses so that you can factor that into your total sum of fixed expenses. For example, if you have a car insurance policy that you make two annual payments for, then you would divide the cost of one semi-annual payment by six to determine how much that policy costs you per single month. To illustrate, a semi-annual car insurance payment of $630 would cost $105 per month. In this hypothetical scenario, a budgeter would include $105 for car insurance as a fixed expense in their left-hand column. When you have exhaustively accounted for every fixed expense in your life, including those which occur on an infrequent basis, listed them, and added up their total monthly cost to you, you are done with the first of your budget's three columns, provided that you are not struggling to pay off any outstanding debts.

However, you might be in debt. If that is the case, you should start trying to figure out what you need to do in order to pay off your outstanding debts. The budget is the perfect tool for doing that. First, determine how soon you want your debts paid off. For sake of simplicity, this hypothetical example will assume that your financial goals include living debt-free within twelve months. In that case, you would calculate how much money you will need to set aside on a monthly basis in order to reach your goal of paying off balances in a given period of time. So, divide the remaining balance of your outstanding debts by twelve; this quotient represents your monthly fixed expense that will go towards the paying off of debts. Make sure that you factor in the accrual of interest as well.

The middle column of your budget is for variable expenses. These are expenses that occur with regular, predictable frequency, but in varying amounts each time. Common household variable expenses include utilities, groceries, gasoline, entertainment, and clothing. When creating your list of variable expenses, be honest with yourself. Did you lose a bill at the blackjack table one night? Include that as an expense. Perhaps you caved and bought a bottle of wine. That counts as a variable expense, too. Like you did with your fixed expenses, calculate how much money your variable expenses are costing you each month. List them all out and add them up.

Next, add up the totals of the first and middle columns so that you have a cumulative total dollar amount that reflects your total monthly expenses. Write this figure in large print so that it stretches and occupies space near the bottoms of both of the two columns of expenses. That extra large number is the number that you have to beat. This looming figure signifies the amount of money that your earnings must exceed if you are going to make strides towards your financial goals. A budget will help you keep track of your spending so that you might bring your total expenses down.

Finally, move on to your budget's right-hand column. This final column will contain your incomes. Using one horizontal line per item, list out each income source that you earned or anticipate earning this month along with its corresponding dollar amount. Include every income source that you can possibly think of, including paychecks, gifts, alimony payments, refunds, interest, and rebates. When you have taken an exhaustive inventory of your income sources and documented them in your budget's rightmost column, then you are ready to calculate your total monthly income.

To do so, simply add up the values of all of your sources of income together. Write this sum in large print near the bottom of your budget's income column. When you do this, go ahead and immediately compare your total income figure to that of your total expenses. Does your total income exceed your monthly expenses, including payments towards existing debts? If so, then you are well on your way towards financial stability. On the other hand, if your total expenses exceed your total income, then you will need to make adjustments to your budget so that you might move towards financial stability.

For example, many new budgeters find themselves surprised to discover how much money they spend on unnecessary goods and services. When my fiancée and I first made our budget, I was embarrassed to realize how much money I was throwing away on unneeded products like sit-down dinners with friends, gasoline for walking-distance trips, and even cheap wine. Thankfully, having a written, documented budget afforded me the opportunity to see exactly where my extra income was going. As such, I found it rather easy to make small adaptations to my lifestyle that would increase the balance of my checking account over time. I still enjoyed many of the same activities that I did before, only with small adjustments. For example, instead of going out to dinner with my friends every weekend like I did before, I would instead offer to cook a homemade meal for my inner social circle. I actually found that it cost slightly less to feed five individuals at home than it does to buy one sit-down meal, including tax and tip. My friends even ended up helping out and bringing some ingredients to my apartment for our weekly dinners together. Furthermore, I began to skate, walk, or use my bicycle for shorter trips instead of driving. Not only did I save money on gasoline and car maintenance, I also noticed improvements in my physical fitness as a result. I cut back on drinking, too. I probably would have never thought to make these money-saving adjustments to my lifestyle if I had not seen my itemized budget in front of me.

In sum, a well-composed, adjustable, three-columned budget will help you visualize the sources of all of your expenses and incomes. You will want to find the sums of your fixed expenses, variable expenses, and incomes so that you can determine how you are doing in terms of money management.

In addendum, budgeters need to make adjustments as they go. A budget is a living document. It is not a list that you make once and then forget about. To illustrate, if you get a bonus at work, then you will need to add that to your incomes column for the month in which you receive it. Then, assuming that you do not receive it again for a while, remove that item from your budget on the first day of the following month. Expert budgeters refer to and update their respective working budgets at least once a week.

Saving

In addition to budgeting, saving will also help you hold on to more of your money as you earn it. Making more money will do you no good if you fail to save any of it. For the purposes of this section, saving does not refer to receiving discounts. For example, many grocery coupons will advertise deals like "save fifty cents," "save fifteen percent," and the like. Of course, using coupons is a useful money management tactic. However, this section does not cover that type of saving. Rather, it will focus on the act of putting money away and holding on to it for when it is needed most. If you do not save any money, then you will not improve your net worth.

First, many well-known banks offer customers automatic savings programs. For example, U.S. Bank's Savings Today And Rewards Tomorrow (S.T.A.R.T.) program works in such a way that it automatically transfers twenty-five dollars from the customer's checking account to their savings account on a recurring monthly basis. The customer has the power to choose exactly which day of the month this transfer occurs on. This program assumes that the customer will not immediately withdraw the transferred funds from the savings account; most banks do not encourage the linking of a debit card to a savings account. Check with your bank of choice to see if they have a savings program that is right for you.

Second, if you can afford to do so, include savings in your budget. As you go about your money management endeavors, you might find yourself with extra money to spare. While there is nothing wrong with spending money on fun things when you can afford to do so, it would be difficult to debate the proposition that saving extra money is the most responsible thing to do with it. As such, consider including "savings" as a variable or fixed expense in your budget. To illustrate, you will be putting money into your savings account so that you do not touch it and lose it immediately. As such, that money is considered an expense, not an income.

Third, if you enjoy the convenience of enrollment in a direct deposit program, see if you can adjust your direct deposits so that your savings account receives a portion of any directly deposited funds. Most major banks allow direct depositors to place a predetermined dollar amount or percentage of their directly deposited paychecks into their savings account while the rest goes into a checking account. You can usually choose whether you want this arrangement to take place temporarily or in perpetuity. One visit to a bank branch can set you up for an entire career of regular, dependable saving.

Fourth, replace paid off debt payments with payments to your savings account. Once you pay off an outstanding debt, you will have extra money as the money that would have otherwise gone towards an existing debt no longer has to be used for that purpose. You can always use that extra income to pay off other debts and potentially save on interest. However, as you reach financial stability, consider placing money that you used to spend on outstanding debts into a savings account. You can even give yourself a small reward for paying off that debt while still saving up. For example, if last month you made your final $200 monthly payment on an outstanding credit card debt, then split that newfound extra money this month between yourself and your savings account. You might consider doing something like placing $140 into savings and spending $60 on something fun for yourself.

Lastly, it will benefit you to place extra, irregular incomes into your savings. For example, birthday checks, workplace bonuses, gifts, and money from odd jobs might make their way into your savings account if doing so is a financially sound decision. However, if you have an outstanding balance on a credit card with a 25% interest rate, then using extra irregular income on your credit card debt is a smarter financial decision than is depositing it into a savings account that earns 1% interest.

The decision to save money in a savings account could make the difference between a financially stable future and a lifetime of money struggles. If you are drowning in debt, the thought of putting money into an account where you are not supposed to touch it might baffle you. However, the act of money management requires both long-term and short-term planning. It may be difficult to think about the future when you are just trying to pay this month's bills, but doing so will be of a great benefit to you when the time comes.

Enjoying your eBook so far? Take a moment to subscribe to our FREE newsletter for incredible discounts, books giveaways, and VIP offers!

> ➢ http://www.connectionbooksclub.com/bonus/

All we need is your email, and you'll be set up to receive more of the eBooks you can't wait to read.

An Active Approach

Unless you can afford the services of professional personal finance managers, personal money management is going to be an ongoing, unending process. Money management is not an event, nor is it an occasion. It is a perpetual activity that one must regularly engage with if they are going to become more financially well off. Two active approaches to money management will help your situation: achieving goals and taking action.

Achieving Goals

In order to achieve your financial goals, you must first set them. Determining your goals is not always going to be an easy task. In order to make an informed decision regarding the prioritization of your financial goals, you must know which actions will provide you with the biggest payoffs. For example, as alluded to earlier, making a payment on a credit card with a 20% interest rate is a smarter decision than making a payment on a credit card with a 10% interest rate that has the same balance. So, organizing your financial documents will greatly assist you in setting appropriate goals, the first step towards achieving them.

When setting your financial goals, it is crucial that you determine what is most important to you personally. Funds are finite; as such, you will have to make choices pertaining to their allocation. For example, many well-meaning individuals prioritize the well-beings of their pets and children over their credit card payments. Such people might spend a little extra money on top-of-the-line dog food at the expense of their ability to pay off their credit card bill in a timely manner, to illustrate. While you should aim to end up debt free and with a positive net worth, the determination of your priorities will help you set your financial goals.

As an exercise, create a list of the most important money-costing aspects of your life. For example, you might include on this list survival, children, pets, rent, and vehicle. Next, rank them in terms of importance. You will strive to achieve every item on this list; the order in which you rank them will help you determine the order in which you strive to satisfy these goals. As such, you might give yourself a few extra months to pay off a hospital bill if it means ensuring that you and your dog have adequate food every night.

In order to achieve your goals, you will need discipline. The establishment of financial goals themselves will afford you focus. Now, it is up to you to dedicate yourself to the realization of those goals. Do not cheat yourself. When I was in college, I was never rich, but I did manage to stay out of debt the entire time. Meanwhile, I watched as one of my hard-working peers constantly complained about her financial situation but refused to exercise a healthy dose of discretion in her spending. She would regularly spend upwards of fifty dollars a week on cigarettes and top-shelf liquor alone. Then, she often went out to the mall with friends and spent money on new clothes that she did not need. She obviously valued her vices more than her financial well-being. If you intend to achieve financial goals, do not make the same mistakes that my friend and many other unfortunate college students make.

In order to reach your money management goals, you will need to stick to a budget, be honest with yourself, and constantly seek new ways to save money.

Taking Action

You will not reach your financial goals by sitting in your home, wallowing in sorrow over your situation. Instead, you must take an active approach towards money management. Action makes the difference between wealthy and would-be well-off.

So, get to work!

First, pick up the phone and make the calls that you need to make. If you have an outstanding credit card balance that overwhelms you, call your bank and ask about transferring the balance to a card with a lower interest rate. If you think you would benefit from a debt consolidation loan, get on the phone with your preferred creditor and inquire about such a loan. You will not get anywhere lying in bed feeling sorry for yourself. Nobody is going to come to your rescue. The power to turn your financial life around lies in your hands.

Next, stay on top of your budget. You will almost certainly have variable expenses that need changing every month. When budget-related variables arise, add them into your budget. Then, make adjustments to your spending habits as necessary. You cannot craft one budget and then expect it to hold true for months to come. Your expenses and incomes will, in all likelihood, vary from month to month. It is up to you to reflect those variations in your budget as they occur.

Only when you have set up automated payments for all of your outstanding and anticipated debts, enrolled in a direct deposit savings program, and applied as many automations as reasonably possible to your financial transactions can you at all take a passive approach to money management.

In the past, humans did not always have the luxury of surviving by taking a passive approach to their assets. Consider the evolutionary implications of financial management. Dozens of thousands of years ago, our tribal ancestors did not enjoy things like credit cards and loans that allowed them to survive while not having any net worth. In the event that a tribal human ran out of essential assets like food or precious metals with which to barter for food, then his or her survival instinct would prompt them to acquire the resources that they needed in order to survive another day. For example, if a tribal man got hungry, but had no food in his possession, then hunger would motivate him to seek out food. If that person could not acquire food, either by finding it or bartering for it, then that person would die. In other words, the tribal version of debt weeded out of the gene pool those who had poor "money" management abilities.

However, today's modern society allows humans to acquire necessities like food without actually having the means to pay for it. Consumers can buy products on credit cards now and not have to worry about paying for those purchases until next month. In a sense, contemporary financial institutions have encouraged the modern human to take a more passive approach to paying off debts. Do not be misled by the convenience of contemporary creditors. Stay on top of your finances by taking action.

Also, you are not going to climb the ladder of success if you constantly blame others for your shortcomings. A deceased relative might have left you with debts; you might have lost some assets in a lawsuit; perhaps you suffered an unfortunate injury and are now facing very expensive hospital bills. The world might deal you a poor hand. Still, your financial situation is your responsibility, even though it might not necessarily be your fault. The sooner you realize this, the better off you will be. If you wallow in misery, angry at the world for the undesirable financial situation that it left you with, you are not doing yourself any favors. Taking responsibility is the first step in taking action.

Of course, if you live in a country where the national leaders hoard all of the wealth for themselves, then you might have a valid excuse for any financial instability that you might experience. However, most Western nations are rampant with financial opportunity for anyone willing to put in the work.

Enjoying your eBook so far? Take a moment to subscribe to our FREE newsletter for incredible discounts, books giveaways, and VIP offers!

- http://www.connectionbooksclub.com/bonus/

All we need is your email, and you'll be set up to receive more of the eBooks you can't wait to read.

Investing In Your Future

Most people find it difficult to plan for the future when they are barely able to pay off this month's expenses. Unfortunately, the future tends to come quickly. It will be in your best interest to begin preparing yourself for a future of financial stability today. As mentioned earlier, putting away money in a savings account will greatly assist anyone's financial future. This chapter will cover more strategies for investing in the future, including retirement accounts. Many types of retirement accounts exist. In addition, you can invest in your future by buying bonds, highly reliable investments.

Retirement Accounts

Retirement is the time period during which you relax and enjoy the fruits of your labor. Most people retire after or around the time that they become senior citizens. During retirement, people do not work full-time jobs. They usually rely on the money that they have saved in a retirement account in order to sustain themselves. This section will cover the most common types of retirement accounts, their benefits, and their potential drawbacks. Investing regularly in a retirement account will provide you a future of financial stability.

First, most full-time employers offer their employees the option to invest in a 401(k) account. Such programs automatically deduct a predetermined amount of money from each of your paychecks. Those deductions go into an account where they are held until your retirement, at which point you have access to them. The money that gets deducted from your paychecks and placed into your 401(k) is not subject to income taxes. In other words, you get away with not paying taxes on a portion of your income if you are willing to wait many years for non-penalized access to it. In the event that you need to withdraw money from your 401(k) before you reach retirement, you can usually do so, but you will most likely have to pay a penalty fee in exchange for your early access to those funds. In some cases, employers will match all of or a portion of your contributions to your own 401(k). That means that for every investment that you make into your retirement account, your employer will also invest into it. Consult with your workplace's higher-ups for more information about their 401(k) program.

Second, some workplaces offer employees a 403(b) retirement plan. A 403(b) works similarly to a 401(k). In fact, the two are almost identical in how they operate. The key difference between a 401(k) and a 403(b) comes in the form of the workplaces that offer them. While most for-profit businesses tend to offer 401(k)s, 403(b)s are most commonly provided to employees in the nonprofit sector, such as teachers and religious leaders.

Alternatively, you might be self-employed. If that is the case, you can still establish a 401(k) for yourself. Such a retirement plan is known as a sole 401(k). Under the terms of a sole 401(k), the owner of the plan acts as both the employer and the employee, meaning that they can match their own contributions. Neither contributions made as an employer or as an employee are subject to income taxes. This is helpful because federal regulations place limits on the total amount of 401(k) contributions that can receive income tax exemptions.

Fourth, one might wish to invest in an individual retirement account. Commonly abbreviated as IRA, an individual retirement account allows you or anyone else to make tax-exempt contributions to the account in amounts of up to several thousand dollars per year. IRAs are ideal choices for individuals whose incomes lie below America's ninetieth income percentile or do not have retirement accounts established with their respective places of employment. Regulations dictate that if a single person earns an amount greater than $71000 in the course of one calendar year, then their IRA contributions do not qualify as tax-deductible income. On the other hand, if your workplace does not provide you with a retirement plan, then your IRA contributions are tax-exempt, no matter how much money you make in a span of twelve months.

Fifth, along those same lines, you might be interested in an alternative form of an individual retirement account known as a simple IRA. Under the terms of a simple IRA, an employer who employs employees in a quantity of less than one hundred at a time can establish retirement accounts for all of his or her subordinates. Simple IRAs require significantly less paperwork to establish than do traditional individual retirement accounts. They require the employer to either match all employee contributions or contribute amounts that go beyond matching. Small businesses often choose to provide their employees with simple IRAs because of the simplicity involved in setting up such a program.

Also, if you are self-employed and interested in an IRA, then you have the ability to establish for yourself a SEP IRA. Also known as a self-employed pension individual retirement account, SEP IRAs give self-employed persons the chance to make tax-exempt contributions to their own retirement accounts. Like simple IRAs, SEP IRAs typically involve a much less complex setup process than do traditional IRAs.

Seventh, a health savings account makes itself an attractive choice of retirement plans for those with high-deductible health insurance plans. Health savings accounts allow individuals to make withdraws at any time in order to pay for medical expenses. Some also allow for the use of funds on dental and vision-related expenses. The balance of a health savings account never expires; it carries over from year to year perpetually and indefinitely. Once the owner of a health savings account turns 59.5 years old, then they are free to withdraw money from their health savings account for any purpose. However, money withdrawn from such an account for purposes other than health-related expenses is subject to taxation.

Many factors will determine whether you should invest in a retirement account and when. If you live a particularly risky or unhealthy lifestyle and do not anticipate living beyond your fifties or sixties, then a retirement account may not be a wise investment for your personal situation. On the other hand, if you plan on living a safe, healthy life of longevity, then you should consider a retirement account. Your options include a 401(k), a 403(b), a sole 401(k), an individual retirement account, a simple individual retirement account, a self-employed pension individual retirement account, a health savings account, and many other, less common varieties not covered in this book.

Bonds

Bonds work like formal versions of I.O.U.s. Under the terms of a bond, you, the investor, agree to loan to a formal organization such as a corporation or government a sum of money. In exchange, that entity is responsible for paying you back the entire amount of that loan plus interest on a predetermined date in the future. The exact terms of these agreements that deal with amounts loaned, interest rates paid, and maturation dates vary from bond to bond. Bonds are generally considered a safe investment.

If you can spare some money for bonds now, consider investing in them, especially if you find ones with interest rates greater than the current rate of inflation. As with all financial decisions, be sure to incorporate any bond purchases and payoffs into your budget each month.

Enjoying your eBook so far? Take a moment to subscribe to our FREE newsletter for incredible discounts, books giveaways, and VIP offers!

> ➤ http://www.connectionbooksclub.com/bonus/

All we need is your email, and you'll be set up to receive more of the eBooks you can't wait to read.

Relationships And Money

Romantic relationships add an entirely new dimension to money management strategies. When you get married or move in with a partner, your financial standing changes in the eyes of governing bodies. To illustrate, married individuals often pay fewer taxes and enjoy looser regulations on their retirement accounts than do single working people. This chapter is designed to assist readers in managing their money in the face of a committed romantic relationship.

When you and your committed long-term partner go about your money management strategies, it is important to do so as a team. If you intend to spend the rest of your foreseeable future with another living individual, then you and your partner must make informed spending decisions together.

Half is Theirs

When you get married, unless you formally agree otherwise ahead of time, half of the money acquired during a marriage belongs to either spouse. To illustrate, when couples divorce, it is customary for the courts to award a considerable portion of the couple's combined net worth to each divorcee. When and if you get married, understand from the start that half of any money that you earn while you are married belongs to your spouse, and vice-versa. Even if your spouse does not work a single day in his or her life while you hold down a full-time job for the entirety of your marriage, one-half of that income still belongs to the other participant in your marriage. If you are unwilling to accept such terms, either get a prenuptial agreement or avoid holy union.

I do not wish to tell you how to go about your romantic endeavors, especially in the pages of a book about money management. However, I would recommend to anyone concerned about their own finances that they only get married to somebody whom they can wholly trust with money. Getting married to an untrustworthy or financially irresponsible person might prove disastrous for one or both spouses involved.

Nevertheless, experts recommend that you and your spouse combine finances upon getting married. Do away with your individual bank accounts, as well as those which your spouse has sole control over; withdraw and combine your balances into one shared, joint account. While you might be frightened at the thought of handing one-half of the financial decision-making power over to another person, the formal combination of finances between two married individuals will breed numerous benefits for both spouses involved.

The first, immediately noticeable benefit of doing away with individual accounts comes in the form of convenience. If either you or your spouse has their own assets that the other has no access to, then the both of you have to file federal tax forms for your own accounts. On the other hand, a joint account means less paperwork between the two of you.

Second, establishing a shared responsibility for all financial assets signifies trust. According to Gottman certified couple's therapist Michael McNulty, the willingness and ability to combine finances are huge indicators of a strong bond between partners. When you and your spouse formally assume shared power over each of your bank accounts, you both demonstrate that you are thinking about a lasting future together. To elaborate, this action strongly suggests that you trust your spouse's ability to handle money well, and vice-versa.

Along those same lines, equally or perhaps more important than your decision to establish a joint bank account is your decision to have that conversation. A marriage counselor can help direct that conversation to its end if you and your spouse wish to make use of such services. Family therapists recommend that couples undergo at least one counseling session before their wedding date to discuss matters that pertain to the combination of assets.

At these sessions, prospective newlyweds can expect for the therapist or counselor to prompt each hopeful spouse to open up about their feelings towards financial matters. It is during this time that partners tend to reveal the sources of their attitudes towards money. For example, during couple's counseling sessions, men and women commonly share details regarding how their own families handled money whilst they were growing up.

To sum up, when you and your spouse eagerly combine responsibility of all assets involved in the marriage, you will enjoy tax benefits, convenience, and a more trustful relationship.

When to Not Join Accounts

Even though you and your spouse might have the best intentions in establishing one joint bank account, there are certain circumstances that usually render that action unwise.

To illustrate, if either you or your spouse is involved in an inheritance, then you should not combine all of your assets. Heirs typically wish to ensure that the money involved in their inheritances does not exit their respective bloodlines. In the event that the couple gets a divorce, then one-half of an inheritance could very well end up in the wrongful hands of a vindictive ex-spouse.

Furthermore, it would not make sense to combine assets if either you or your spouse already has a child over which they have custody. In order to prevent the wrongful use of child support payments, courts forbid new spouses from accessing child support payments from an ex-spouse. The judicial system ensures that the child support money that payer pays goes to its rightful source: the child. If you and your new spouse do decide to combine accounts while one or both of you receives child support payments, the judge may terminate your ex's obligation to continue making those payments.

Lastly, if one spouse is markedly better at handling money responsibly than the other, then you may wish to avoid the combination of bank balances. Assuming that you and your spouse can have this conversation maturely, it may be of immense benefit to your financial situation if you formally agree to let the more financially responsible partner assume majority or sole control over your finances. Remember, in the event of a divorce, the courts will assume that each spouse owns fifty percent of your total combined net worth as a couple. You want to prepare yourself for the worst while you strive for the best with regards to your marriage and its financial implications. If you begin to identify personally with your level of control over your marriage's finances, then your ego stands to get in the way of your ability to make decisions that lead to the best possible outcome for your financial situation. In other words, if you characteristically struggle with money, then it may be worthwhile to sacrifice to your more financially responsible spouse some shared control over your marriage's finances in order to better your financial situation.

Work Together

If you and your spouse are ready to take your collaborative money management efforts to the next level, work together on creating your joint budget. The combined budgeting powers of you and your spouse are greater than the sum of their parts. What one spouse glosses over, the other may know how to examine in depth. You can catch each other's mistakes, inform one another of anything left out, and keep one another in check with regards to spending habits.

Working together on a budget breeds a sense of shared responsibility between spouses. It also lends itself to trust; each spouse reveals to one another the entireties of their incomes and expenses. When all costs and acquisitions are laid out on the table, partners in marriage will have the ability to keep tabs on the honesty levels of each other. A joint budget provides each partner with knowledge regarding how much money to expect in the bank account at any given time. If money mysteriously goes missing, then the answer to that mystery will be more easily revealed with an itemized budget providing the couple with a thorough method for tracking every dollar that comes in and out of their shared account.

Dear Reader,

Connection Books Club wants to thank you for the purchase of one of our many informative eBooks! We hope you enjoyed your purchase and we want to invite you to join our club.

When you subscribe to our FREE club, you'll receive regular newsletters and incredible discounts on our bestselling books! Connection Books Club makes reading easy, giving you the content you want, at a price you can't believe. All that it takes to enroll in our FREE book club is your email. We'll send you the latest business and personal development news and highlight the newest books that are ready for you to enjoy.

http://www.connectionbooksclub.com/bonus/

By subscribing to Connection Books Club, not only will you get incredible discounts, a regular newsletter, but you'll also get the opportunity to receive FREE eBooks! Subscribers are invited to share reviews of the eBooks they've read, earning new titles at no cost! All it takes to enroll is your email.
http://www.connectionbooksclub.com/bonus/

Discounts and free eBooks are just a click away! Enter your email for VIP access to new books, incredible deals and money saving options, and even free giveaways! And don't forget, by signing up today for Connection Books Club, you'll receive the incredible eBook *Money Management: Learn How to Organize Your Financial Life and Invest in Your Future* for FREE!

Connection Books Club is excited to have you join our ranks of subscribers. We hope you enjoy your FREE eBook and all the great reading coming your way soon!

http://www.connectionbooksclub.com/bonus/

Conclusion

Thank for making it through to the end of *Money Management: Learn How to Organize Your Financial Life and Invest in Your Future*. I wrote this book with a desire that readers find it useful, practical, and informative. I hope that you feel confident that you have the tools and ability to reach your financial goals, whatever those might be. Revisit chapter 4 for a refresher on financial goals.

The next step is to put yourself to work and continue your diligent money management efforts. The fact that you read this book through to the end provides a testament to your dedication to building wealth. Unless you are a fortunate heir or underage child, nobody is going to take responsibility for your financial situation unless you pay them to. Even then, that money would be better spent on yourself, through saving, investing, or paying off debts.

While limits to the amount of money that you can acquire might technically exist, some brilliant people have made huge fortunes for themselves within those limitations. In fact, some successful American individuals earn hundreds of millions of dollars annually. Our wealthy predecessors have already proven what is possible. There is no reason why you cannot live up to that. With a savvy mind, a thorough approach, and strict discipline, you can build wealth in ways that you never thought possible.

Finally, if you found this book useful in any way, a review on Amazon is always appreciated! Happy money managing!

www.ingramcontent.com/pod-product-compliance
Lightning Source LLC
Chambersburg PA
CBHW050027230526
45470CB00003B/1166